hearty soups

hearty soups

delicious meals in a bowl

RYLAND
PETERS
& SMALL

LONDON NEW YORK

Designer Luana Gobbo
Editor Rachel Lawrence
Production Simon Walsh
Art Director Anne-Marie Bulat
Publishing Director Alison Starling
Indexer Hilary Bird

First published in the United Kingdom in 2006
by Ryland Peters & Small
20–21 Jockey's Fields
London WC1R 4BW
www.rylandpeters.com

10 9 8 7 6 5 4 3 2

Recipes © Maxine Clark, Clare Ferguson,
Manisha Gambhir Harkins, Elsa Petersen-
Schepelern, Laura Washburn 2006
Design and photographs
© Ryland Peters & Small 2006

ISBN-10: 1 84597 221 X
ISBN-13: 978 1 84597 221 9

A CIP catalogue record for this book is available
from the British Library.

Printed and bound in China.

Notes

All spoon measurements are level.

All eggs are medium, unless otherwise specified.
Uncooked or partly cooked eggs should not
be served to the very young, the very old,
those with compromised immune systems,
or to pregnant women.

contents

a meal in a bowl

Soup is one of the simplest and most universal dishes and has been a staple meal in many parts of the world throughout history. The word dates back to medieval times when broth was poured over a piece of bread known as a 'sop'. Soups were traditionally a cheap and easy way of cooking whatever ingredients were locally available – from the Mediterranean fish of the French classic bouillabaisse to the aromatic herbs and spices of South-east Asian soups.

The wonderful thing about soup is its versatility. Most recipes follow the same basic method, allowing you to experiment with different ingredients and flavourings or simply use whatever is in your refrigerator. Many of the recipes in this book feature irresistible additions, such as cheese-topped croutes or tortilla wedges, which really turn a soup into a meal.

Good-quality stock is essential in soup and it is certainly worth the effort of making your own, following the recipes on pages 8–9, and you can always make extra and freeze it for later use. If you're really pushed for time, ready-made fresh stocks are available and there's nothing wrong with keeping some good-quality stock cubes or powder in your cupboard as a stand-by. Packed with goodness and flavour, a hearty soup is a meal in itself and you are sure to discover a few favourites in this delicious collection of recipes.

stocks

beef stock

2 kg beef bones

40 g unsalted butter or oil
(not olive oil) or a mixture of both

500 g stewing beef,
cut into 2 cm cubes

2 large onions, chopped

2 large carrots, chopped

a small handful of parsley,
stalks bruised

1 tablespoon black peppercorns,
lightly crushed

1 leek, halved and chopped

2 celery stalks, thinly sliced

1 bouquet garni (a bunch of herbs
tied up with kitchen string)

makes about 2 litres

To make basic beef stock, put all the ingredients in a large stockpot, cover with 4 litres water and bring to the boil. Reduce the heat to a simmer. For the first 30 minutes, you must skim off the foam that rises to the surface. This will help make the stock clearer and less fatty. It should be just hot enough to let a large, slow bubble break on the surface of the liquid. Do not let it boil, or the fat will be constantly redistributed through the stock.

When cooking is complete, remove from the heat and strain through a colander into a large bowl. Discard the solids. Let the stock cool, then transfer to the refrigerator, cover and chill overnight. The next morning, scrape off the fat that will have risen to the top.

Strain through a fine sieve, then ladle into conveniently sized containers: 1 litre will serve 4 people.

If you are left with a little stock that's not enough for a whole recipe, pour it into ice cube trays, freeze, then keep the cubes in freezer bags – whenever you need 'a tablespoon of stock', the cube equals about a tablespoon.

chicken stock

2 kg chicken carcasses, wings or drumsticks
or a whole chicken

2 onions, chopped

2 carrots, chopped

1 celery stalk, chopped

a few sprigs of parsley, stalks bruised

2 tablespoons peppercorns, lightly crushed

1 fresh bay leaf, or ½ dried

1 leek, halved and chopped

makes 2 litres

Put all the ingredients in a large stockpot, add 3 litres water and bring to the boil. As the water heats, skim off the foam from time to time. Reduce to simmering and cook, uncovered, for at least 4 hours. Skim off the foam as it accumulates.

Strain the stock through a colander into a bowl, let cool, then chill in the refrigerator overnight. Next day, scrape off the fat that has risen to the top. Decant into 1 litre containers, then freeze.

vegetable stock

2 garlic cloves, crushed

1 large onion, chopped

3 large leeks, halved and chopped

2 large carrots, chopped

2 celery stalks, chopped

40 g unsalted butter, melted

1 tablespoon olive oil

250 ml white wine

a handful of parsley stalks, lightly crushed

2 bay leaves

a sprig of thyme

makes 1 litre

Put all the vegetables in a plastic bag, then add the butter and olive oil and shake the bag so everything is evenly coated. Remove the vegetables from the bag and transfer to a roasting tin, extracting every last drop of oil from the bag. Roast in a preheated oven at 200°C (400°F) Gas 6 for 40–45 minutes, turning from time to time, then transfer to a stockpot. Put the empty tin on top of the stove and add the wine and 500 ml water. Scrape up any residues from the tin and pour these into the stockpot.

Add 2½ litres water, the parsley stalks, bay leaves and thyme, and bring to the boil. Reduce the heat, cover with a lid and let simmer for 1 hour. Remove from the heat and let cool.

Strain the stock through a fine sieve and discard the vegetables and flavourings. Pour the stock back into the rinsed pan and bring to the boil. Keep boiling until reduced by half. Use immediately or let cool and use within 2 days, or freeze.

fish stock

2 kg heads and frames of white fish

75 g unsalted butter

2 onions, very finely chopped

1 carrot, very finely chopped

1 small celery stalk, very finely chopped

1 small leek, halved and very finely chopped

1 teaspoon peppercorns

a few sprigs of parsley, stalks bruised, then finely chopped

150 ml white wine

1 litre iced water and ice cubes

makes 1 litre

First, trim the gills out of the fish heads (or get a fishmonger to do it for you) as these make stock bitter.

Melt the butter in a large saucepan or stockpot, then add the onions, carrot, celery, leek, peppercorns and parsley and cook gently until softened and translucent. Don't let it brown. Add the wine and bring to the boil, then add the iced water and ice cubes. The butter will stick to the ice cubes and you can remove them. Add the fish heads and frames, bring to the boil again, reduce the heat and simmer for 30 minutes, skimming occasionally. Remove from the heat and strain out the solids. Strain again through a fine sieve.

Return the stock to the rinsed saucepan and return to the boil. Simmer until reduced by about a third or a half, to intensify the flavour. Use immediately, or let cool, then chill. When cold, decant into small containers, about 250–500 ml each.

vegetables

french onion soup

This was the porters' favourite dish in the great Paris market of Les Halles. Although the market relocated to the Parisian suburbs in the 1960s, there are still restaurants near the original site serving bowls of this fortifying brew. Take care to let it cool slightly before eating as it can be extremely hot!

Put the butter and olive oil in a large saucepan or stockpot and heat until the butter melts. Add the onions and salt and stir well. Cook over low heat for 20–30 minutes or until the onions are golden brown. Do not increase the heat, or the butter will burn. Sprinkle the flour over the onions and stir for 2–3 minutes until there is no sign of white specks of flour (if you leave them, they will appear as lumps in the final soup).

Heat the stock in a separate saucepan, then pour 1–2 ladles onto the onions. Stir well, then add the remaining stock and simmer, part-covered, for another 20–30 minutes. Add salt and pepper to taste.

Meanwhile, put the bread on a baking sheet and toast in a preheated oven at 160°C (325°F) Gas 3 for about 15 minutes. Brush with the olive oil and rub with the cut garlic clove, return to the oven for another 15 minutes or until the bread is quite dry (if you put undried bread in the soup it will turn to mush).

To serve, ladle the soup into 6 onion soup bowls.* Put the slices of toast (the croutes) on top and pile the cheese over them. Dot with butter and cook at the same temperature for about 15 minutes until the cheese is melted. Put under a preheated grill to brown the top for 1–2 minutes if you like.

*Note The little bowls shown here, with pedestal foot and lion's head handles, are the traditional onion soup dishes, made by Pillivuyt and Apilco, two of the great French porcelain makers. Use a dessert spoon to eat from them – a soup spoon is too big.

50 g unsalted butter, preferably clarified, plus extra butter to serve

1 tablespoon olive oil

1 kg onions, thinly sliced

1 teaspoon sea salt, plus extra to taste

50 g plain flour

1 litre Beef or Chicken Stock (page 8)

freshly ground black pepper

to serve

8–12 thick slices of bread (about 2 cm)

1 tablespoon olive oil

1 large garlic clove, halved

125 g freshly grated Gruyère cheese

serves 4–6

vegetable bouillabaisse

4 tablespoons extra virgin olive oil

2 leeks, white part only, halved lengthways, then sliced crossways

1 large onion, chopped

1 fennel bulb, halved, cored and chopped

3 garlic cloves, crushed

3 large ripe tomatoes, skinned, deseeded and chopped

5 medium new potatoes, cubed

1 teaspoon sea salt, plus extra to taste

2 litres Vegetable Stock (page 9) or water

1 fresh bay leaf

a sprig of thyme

a strip of zest from 1 unwaxed orange

1 teaspoon good-quality saffron strands

1 baguette loaf, sliced, for croutons

100 g freshly grated Gruyère cheese

freshly ground black pepper

a handful of flat leaf parsley, chopped, to serve

rouille

3 garlic cloves, very finely chopped

1–2 red chillies, deseeded and very finely chopped

1 egg yolk, at room temperature

about 300 ml extra virgin olive oil

fine sea salt and freshly ground black pepper

serves 4–6

It is difficult to make true bouillabaisse outside France because so many of the fish used are found only in the Mediterranean. But here's a very good vegetable-only alternative with similar flavours, including the best part – the chilli-spiked rouille sauce. Traditional versions include a poached egg, which you may wish to add.

Heat the olive oil in a large saucepan. Add the leeks, onion and fennel and cook until just beginning to brown, about 10 minutes. Stir in the garlic, tomatoes, potatoes and salt and cook for 1 minute. Add the stock, the bay leaf, thyme, orange zest and saffron and stir. Bring to the boil, reduce the heat and simmer gently until the potatoes are tender, about 40 minutes. Add salt and pepper to taste, cover and let stand for at least 1 hour, or cool and refrigerate overnight.

Meanwhile, make the croutons. Arrange the baguette slices in a single layer on a baking sheet. Bake in a preheated oven at 180°C (350°F) Gas 4 until golden, about 5–8 minutes. Set aside.

To make the rouille, put the garlic, chillies and egg yolk in a small, deep bowl. Beat well. Add the olive oil bit by bit and beating vigorously, until the mixture is thick like mayonnaise. Add fine salt and pepper to taste.

To serve, warm the soup if necessary. Put 2–3 croutons in each soup plate, sprinkle with the cheese and ladle in the soup. Sprinkle with parsley and serve with the rouille, to be stirred in according to taste.

green vegetable soup

1 fresh bay leaf

1 small cabbage, quartered

60 g unsalted butter

2 leeks, halved and sliced

1 onion, chopped

2 teaspoons sea salt,
plus extra to taste

250 g new potatoes, chopped

a handful of flat leaf parsley, chopped

250 g fresh shelled peas

1 Little Gem lettuce,
quartered and thinly sliced

a bunch of sorrel, sliced

unsalted butter and/or crème fraîche,
to serve (optional)

freshly ground black pepper

serves 4–6

An old-fashioned nourishing soup, full of healthy green things. The fresh herbs add a delicious flavour, but if you are not able to get hold of any sorrel, simply omit it.

Put the bay leaf in a large saucepan of water and bring to the boil. Add the cabbage quarters and blanch for 3 minutes. Drain the cabbage, pat dry and slice it thinly.

Heat the butter in a large saucepan. Add the blanched cabbage, leeks, onion and salt and cook until softened, 5–10 minutes. Add the potatoes, parsley, 2 litres water, and salt and pepper to taste. Simmer gently for 40 minutes.

Stir in the peas, lettuce and sorrel and cook for 10 minutes more. Taste for seasoning. Ladle into bowls, add 1 tablespoon of butter and/or crème fraîche, if liked, to each and serve.

courgette, corn and cumin soup

3 tablespoons extra virgin olive oil

2 onions, halved, then sliced

3 courgettes, about 600 g, quartered lengthways, then sliced

2–3 potatoes, about 300 g, diced

4 garlic cloves, sliced

2 ears of corn or 250 g fresh or frozen kernels

1 teaspoon ground cumin

1 red chilli, deseeded and sliced

1 litre Chicken or Vegetable Stock (pages 8–9)

sea salt

to serve

crème fraîche or cream

chopped fresh coriander

Tabasco sauce

serves 4

This delicately spicy soup is inspired by the cuisine of America's South-west. Although this combination of vegetables works particularly well, it can be made with whatever vegetables you have in your kitchen. The chilli content is rather conservative, but you can spice it up as much as you like. You can also purée it for a thicker, more chowder-like consistency if you like.

If using fresh ears of corn, remove the husks and silks and cut the stalk end flat. Put the flat end on a board and cut off the kernels from top to bottom. Discard the cobs.

Heat the olive oil in a saucepan. Add the onions, courgettes, potatoes and some salt and cook over high heat until the vegetables begin to brown, about 5 minutes.

Add the garlic, corn, cumin and chilli and cook, stirring, for 1 minute more. Add the stock and 250 ml water, then add salt to taste. Bring to the boil, then lower the heat and simmer gently until the potatoes are tender, 15–20 minutes. Set aside for at least 30 minutes.

To serve, reheat the soup. Ladle into soup bowls and top each with a spoonful of crème fraîche, some coriander and a dash of Tabasco sauce. Serve immediately.

Note For a light meal, put some flour tortillas on a baking sheet, top with grated Cheddar and toast in a hot oven until melted. Cut into wedges to serve with the soup.

la ribollita

250 g dried cannellini beans

150 ml extra virgin olive oil,
plus extra to serve

1 onion, finely chopped

1 carrot, chopped

1 celery stalk, chopped

2 leeks, finely chopped

4 garlic cloves, finely chopped,
plus 1 extra peeled and bruised,
for rubbing

1 small white cabbage, thinly sliced

1 large potato, chopped

4 medium courgettes, chopped

400 ml tomato passata
(strained, crushed tomatoes)

2 sprigs of rosemary

2 sprigs of thyme

2 sprigs of sage

1 dried red chilli

500 g cavolo nero (Tuscan black
cabbage) or Savoy cabbage,
thinly sliced

6 thick slices coarse crusty
white bread

sea salt and freshly ground
black pepper

freshly grated Parmesan cheese,
to serve

serves 8 generously

Best made in large quantities, this is a great soup for a family get-together and is very filling. *Ribollita* means 'reboiled' as the basic bean and vegetable soup is made the day before, then reheated and ladled over toasted garlic bread, sprinkled with olive oil and served with lots of Parmesan cheese.

Put the beans in a bowl, cover with cold water, soak overnight, then drain just before you're ready to use them.

The next day, heat half the olive oil in a large, heavy stockpot, then add the onion, carrot and celery and cook gently for 10 minutes, stirring frequently. Add the leeks and garlic and cook for 10 minutes more. Next, add the white cabbage, potato and courgettes, stir well and cook for 10 minutes, stirring frequently.

Stir in the soaked beans, passata, rosemary, thyme, sage, dried chilli, salt and plenty of black pepper. Cover with about 2 litres water (the vegetables should be well covered), bring to the boil, then turn down the heat and simmer, covered, for at least 2 hours, until the beans are very soft.

Take out 2–3 large ladles of soup and mash well. Stir back into the soup to thicken it. Stir in the cavolo nero and simmer for another 15 minutes.

Remove from the heat, let cool, then refrigerate overnight. The next day, slowly reheat the soup and stir in the remaining olive oil. Toast the bread and rub with garlic. Pile the bread in a tureen or in individual bowls and ladle the soup over the top. Trickle in more olive oil and serve with plenty of freshly grated Parmesan.

soupe au pistou

3 tablespoons extra virgin olive oil

1 onion, chopped

1 small fennel bulb, quartered, cored and chopped

2 courgettes, chopped

200 g new potatoes, chopped

2 tomatoes, skinned, deseeded and chopped

2 litres Vegetable or Chicken stock (pages 8–9)

a sprig of thyme

400 g canned cannellini beans, drained

400 g canned red kidney beans, drained

150 g green beans, cut into 3 cm pieces

50 g spaghetti, broken into pieces

150 g finely grated cheese, such as aged Gouda or Parmesan

coarse sea salt and freshly ground black pepper

pistou

6 garlic cloves

a small bunch of basil, leaves only

6 tablespoons extra virgin olive oil

serves 4–6

This recipe is a version of a well-loved staple of Provençal cuisine. Purists will tell you that only Parisians add carrots and that aged Gouda is imperative. The reason, according to one story, is that this soup was invented by Italian workers building the railway in the hills above Nice, who used the Dutch cheese because there was a lot of it in transit at the port. A variation is to add skinned, deseeded and chopped tomatoes to the pistou.

Heat the olive oil in a large saucepan or casserole dish. Add the onion, fennel and courgettes and cook over medium heat until browned, about 10 minutes. Add the potatoes, tomatoes, stock and thyme. Bring to the boil, then cover and simmer gently for 15 minutes.

Add the cannellini and kidney beans and simmer, covered, for 15 minutes more. Taste and adjust the seasoning with salt and pepper. Add the green beans and the spaghetti and cook until the pasta is tender, about 10 minutes more. Cover and let stand. Ideally, the soup should rest for at least a few hours before serving or, alternatively, you can make it one day in advance and refrigerate it. (Do not make the pistou until you are ready to serve; it is best fresh, and the basil and garlic should not be cooked.)

To make the pistou, put the garlic, basil and olive oil in a small food processor and blend until well chopped. You can also make it using a mortar and pestle – the more authentic method – starting with the garlic and finishing with the oil, added gradually.

Heat the soup and serve with the pistou and cheese, to be stirred in according to taste. The soup can also be served at room temperature.

peas, beans
& lentils

red lentil and chorizo soup

Red lentils are ideal for soups as they cook quickly into a beautifully coloured purée and carry other flavours in a most delicious way. Top them with chorizo, the cooking kind, about 2 cm in diameter – the very spicy ones are often strung with red cord, the sweet ones with white cord. The advantage of using the sweet ones is that you can add other flavours without adding too much pain.

Heat 3 tablespoons of the olive oil in a large saucepan, add the onion, carrot and celery and sauté until softened but not browned. Add the garlic and ginger and sauté until the garlic has softened but is not browned. Stir in the paprika, then add the lentils and stir to cover with the flavourings. Add the stock. Bring to the boil and simmer until the lentils are tender – they will turn into a purée.

Meanwhile, heat the remaining olive oil in a frying pan, add the chorizo slices in a single layer and fry until they are lightly browned, and turn inside out, like tiny bowls. They will be crisp and brown on the underside. Turn them over and lightly fry the other side until crisp. Remove to a plate until ready to serve. Keep the frying oil.

Test the texture of the lentil soup – if too thick, stir in extra boiling stock or water. Ladle into bowls, top with the chorizo and parsley, and spoon the reserved frying oil over the top – it will be a brilliant orange-red.

4 tablespoons olive oil

1 onion, finely chopped

1 large carrot, cubed

1 celery stalk, cubed

2 garlic cloves, crushed

3 cm fresh ginger, grated

½ teaspoon smoked sweet Spanish paprika

500 g red lentils

1 litre Chicken Stock (page 8)

2–3 chorizos (see recipe introduction), thinly sliced

2 tablespoons freshly chopped flat leaf parsley

serves 4

lentil soup with roasted tomatoes and onions

Roasting is the best way to use tomatoes when they are not quite ripe, or so mass-produced as to be flavourless. They go well with lentils, adding great depth of flavour to the broth, and they look good too. The lentils don't require soaking, so after the vegetables have been charred, this becomes a very quick soup.

Put the tomatoes, onion and 2 tablespoons of the olive oil in a baking dish. Toss well and spread to an even layer. Strip the leaves off the herb sprigs and sprinkle over the top. Add a good pinch of salt and roast in a preheated oven at 220°C (425°F) Gas 7 until charred, 20–25 minutes.

Meanwhile, to prepare the lentils, put the remaining olive oil in a large saucepan over medium to high heat. Add the celery, carrot and garlic and cook until just brown and beginning to smell aromatic. Add the stock and 600 ml water. Stir in the lentils, bay leaf and a good pinch of salt. Bring to the boil, then lower the heat, cover and simmer gently until the lentils are tender, 15–20 minutes.

Transfer the roasted tomatoes and onions to a cutting board and chop coarsely. Scrape into the lentil soup. Taste and adjust the seasoning with salt and pepper. Stir in the spinach and parsley and serve with the pepper mill, so people can help themselves.

Variation Add cooked, sliced Italian sausage, 1–2 per person, and this will easily become a main dish.

6 tomatoes, about 500 g, cut into wedges

1 large onion, thickly sliced

3 tablespoons extra virgin olive oil

a few sprigs of herbs, such as thyme, sage or oregano (or 1 tablespoon dried mixed herbs)

2 large celery stalks, chopped

1 large carrot, diced

4 garlic cloves, sliced

1 litre Chicken Stock (page 8)

200 g Puy lentils or other green lentils

1 bay leaf

50 g fresh baby spinach leaves

a handful of flat leaf parsley, chopped

sea salt and freshly ground black pepper

serves 4–6

venetian pea and rice soup with mint

A lovely soup to serve in summer when fresh peas and mint are plentiful. Vialone nano is the favourite risotto rice in the Veneto region of Italy. It is a semi-fino round grain rice, best for soups and risottos, but arborio (a superfino rice used mainly for risottos) will do very nicely. This dish has ancient roots, and was flavoured with fennel seeds at one time. Parsley is more usual now, but mint makes a nice alternative in summer.

Put the stock in a large saucepan and bring it slowly to the boil while you prepare the sautéed sauce.

Heat the olive oil and 30 g of the butter in a large saucepan and, when melted, add the pancetta and spring onion. Cook for about 5 minutes until softened but not browned.

Pour in the rice, stir for a few minutes to toast it, then add the hot stock. Simmer for 10 minutes, stirring from time to time. Add the peas, cook for another 5–7 minutes, then stir in the remaining butter, mint and Parmesan. Add salt and pepper to taste and serve immediately. The rice grains should not be too mushy, and the soup should be thick, but not stodgy.

1.25 litres Chicken, Beef or Vegetable Stock (pages 8–9)

2 tablespoons olive oil

60 g butter

50 g pancetta, finely chopped

white parts of 4 spring onions, finely chopped

200 g Italian risotto rice, preferably vialone nano

1 kg fresh peas in the pod, shelled, or 400 g frozen peas

3 tablespoons freshly chopped mint

freshly grated Parmesan cheese, to taste

sea salt and freshly ground black pepper

serves 4

swedish yellow pea soup

The smoked pork knuckle gives this hearty Scandinavian soup a delicious flavour, but you can replace it with celeriac if you prefer. Simply halve it, peel it carefully and cut into cubes, then add it to the soup at the same time as the peas. For some reason, old Scandinavian cookbooks tell you to soak the peas overnight. You can if you like, but since they're split, they have no coating to be softened so it's not really necessary.

1 smoked pork knuckle or ham hock

500 g yellow split peas

2 onions, halved lengthways

6 cloves, stuck in the onions

1 carrot, thickly sliced

3 fresh bay leaves

3 long curls of orange zest

4 tablespoons Dijon mustard

sea salt (optional) and freshly ground black pepper

scissor-snipped chives or parsley, to serve

serves 4

Put the pork knuckle in a snug-fitting saucepan and cover it with water. Bring to the boil, reduce the heat and simmer until tender. Skim off the foam from time to time and top up with more boiling water as necessary. When done, the meat will fall easily off the bone. Drain, remove the skin and bone and pull the meat into bite-sized shreds, small enough to fit easily on a soup spoon. Reserve 250 ml of the cooking liquid.

Rinse the peas in cold running water and put in a large saucepan. Add the onions stuck with cloves, the carrot, bay leaves, orange zest and 1 litre water. Bring to the boil, reduce the heat and simmer until cooked, about 30 minutes.

The peas should be soft, but still keep their shape. If they are not soft enough, cook for 5–10 minutes more – the time will depend on the age of the peas. Remove the cloves, bay leaves, orange zest and (optional) the onions and carrot. If you would like a smoother texture, the peas can be puréed in a food processor, in batches if necessary.

Return the peas to the saucepan, stir in the mustard and pork shreds and taste for seasoning. Instead of salt, you can add a little of the reserved liquid used to cook the pork. It will be salty and meaty – take care, it's easy to add too much. Serve sprinkled with chives.

minestrone

200 g dried cannellini beans

250 g smoked pancetta or bacon, cut into cubes or strips

2 garlic cloves, crushed

2 large stalks of parsley, lightly crushed

1 tablespoon olive oil

1 large onion, chopped

2 large potatoes, cubed and rinsed

3 carrots, cubed

2 celery stalks, sliced

3 tomatoes, halved, deseeded and chopped

200 g Italian risotto rice

1 small round cabbage, quartered, cored and sliced

250 g shelled peas, fresh or frozen

3 small courgettes, halved lengthways and thickly sliced

sea salt and freshly ground black pepper

to serve

a handful of basil, torn

crusty Italian bread

freshly grated Parmesan cheese

serves 6–8

There are as many versions of minestrone (big soup) as there are regions of Italy and Italian grandmothers. Tomatoes, garlic, oil and pasta are used in southern recipes, beans in soups from central Italy and rice in the north. In Genoa they add a spoonful of pesto, in Tuscany the soup is poured over their chunky unsalted bread, and in other areas, pork or bacon in various forms is added.

Soak the beans overnight in at least 1¼ litres water to cover.

Drain, then put in a saucepan, cover with water and bring to the boil. Reduce the heat and simmer until almost tender (they will be cooked again, so don't let them get too soft). Do not add salt during this precooking, or you will have cannellini bullets. Drain and set aside.

Put the pancetta, garlic and parsley in a stockpot, heat gently and fry until the fat runs. Add the olive oil, heat briefly, then add the onion and cook gently until softened but not browned.

Add the potatoes, carrots, celery, tomatoes, and season with salt and pepper. Add 3 litres water and heat until simmering. Cook over low heat for about 20 minutes. Add the rice and simmer for 10 minutes. Add the cabbage and reserved beans, bring to the boil and cook for 5 minutes, then add the peas and courgettes and cook for another 2–3 minutes until all the vegetables are tender. Remove and discard the parsley stalks, add salt and pepper to taste, then serve sprinkled with basil. Crusty Italian bread and freshly grated Parmesan make the perfect accompaniments.

Note Use canned beans instead of dried if you prefer, but remember that they often have salt and sugar added, so keep that in mind when seasoning the soup. They are already quite soft, so add them at the end and cook only until heated through.

flag bean soup

This is the sort of soup you need on a cold winter's day. The name 'flag soup' was inspired by the red, green and white beans which match the colours of the Italian flag. Using canned beans, it takes no time at all to prepare, and you can use vegetable or chicken stock, according to whether your guests are vegetarian or not.

Heat the olive oil in a frying pan, add the sliced garlic and fry gently on both sides until crisp and golden. Remove and drain on kitchen paper.

Add the onion and crushed garlic to the frying pan, adding extra olive oil if necessary, and cook gently until softened and transparent. Add the lentils and half the boiling stock and cook until the lentils are just tender.

Meanwhile, rinse and drain all the beans. Put them in a sieve and dunk the sieve in a large saucepan of boiling water. The beans are cooked – you are just reheating them.

Add the hot beans to the lentils, then add the remaining stock. Taste, then add salt and pepper as necessary. If the soup is too thick, add extra boiling stock or water. Ladle into bowls, top with the reserved fried garlic and the parsley, add a few drops of olive oil and the lemon zest, if using, then serve with crusty bread.

Note You can use dried beans instead, if you prefer. Soak them overnight and cook for at least 45 minutes, or according to packet instructions.

1 tablespoon olive oil, plus extra to taste

3 large garlic cloves, 2 cut into slices, 1 crushed

1 large onion, finely chopped

250 g Puy lentils

1 litre boiling Chicken or Vegetable Stock (pages 8–9), plus extra to taste

100 g canned butter beans

200 g canned green flageolet beans

200 g canned red kidney beans

200 g canned haricot or cannellini beans

sea salt and freshly ground black pepper

to serve

parsley or basil leaves

grated lemon zest (optional)

crusty bread

serves 4

pasta and bean soup

Italy produces the most wonderful, comforting soups and this one from Campania combines two of the great stand-bys – beans and pasta. This delicious soup is often served in *trattorie* (small family restaurants found all over Italy) and is suprisingly simple to make. Serve with crusty Italian bread, if liked, which is ideal for mopping up the liquid.

185 g dried cannellini or haricot beans

a pinch of bicarbonate of soda

4 tablespoons olive oil, plus extra to serve

2 garlic cloves, crushed

1.75 litres Chicken Stock (page 8) or water

100 g short pasta shapes, such as macaroni or tubetti

4 tomatoes, skinned, deseeded and chopped

4 tablespoons freshly chopped flat leaf parsley

sea salt and freshly ground black pepper

crusty Italian bread, to serve (optional)

serves 6

Put the beans in a bowl, cover with water and add the bicarbonate of soda. Soak overnight, then drain the beans just before you're ready to use them.

The next day, put the drained beans in a large saucepan. Add the olive oil, garlic and stock. Bring to the boil, reduce the heat and simmer, part-covered with a lid, for 1–2 hours or until the beans are tender.

Working it batches if necessary, blend the beans with the cooking liquid using a food processor. Return the bean purée to the rinsed pan, adding extra water or stock as necessary. Add the pasta and simmer gently for 15 minutes until tender. (Add a little extra water or stock if the soup is looking too thick.) Stir in the tomatoes and parsley and season well with salt and pepper. Serve with an extra trickle of olive oil and crusty bread, if liked.

andalusian chickpea soup with chorizo, paprika and saffron

2 tablespoons extra virgin olive oil

1 onion, chopped

3 thin celery stalks, chopped, leaves reserved

1 large carrot, chopped

2 garlic cloves, chopped

250 g chorizo, skinned, halved, then cut into 1 cm slices (or use a mixture of chorizo and another southern European sausage, such as morcilla or fresh small salami)

400 g canned chickpeas, drained

1.75 litres Chicken Stock (page 8)

¼ teaspoon hot pimentón (see recipe introduction)

125 g spinach, tough stalks removed and leaves chopped into large pieces

¼ teaspoon saffron threads, bruised with a mortar and pestle

to serve

Manchego or Parmesan cheese, shaved (optional)

crusty bread (optional)

serves 4

This hearty soup is a meal in itself. Chunks of chorizo and perhaps black pudding (morcilla) or other sausages float alongside chickpeas and spinach in a slightly smoky, fragrant broth. The special flavour comes from two typically Spanish spices, pimentón (Spanish oak-smoked paprika, made from a variety of capsicum or pepper) and its home-grown luxury spice, saffron.

Heat the olive oil in a large saucepan and add the onion, celery and carrot. Gently sauté the vegetables until they begin to soften. Add the garlic, chorizo, chickpeas, stock and pimentón. Bring to the boil, reduce the heat and simmer for about 10 minutes. Add the spinach and celery leaves and simmer for a further 15 minutes.

Add the saffron and clean out the mortar using a little of the stock so as not to waste any of the saffron. Add to the saucepan and simmer for another 5 minutes. Serve hot in large, wide bowls as a main course and top with shavings of cheese, if using. This soup is very filling, but some good crusty bread makes a delightful partner, if liked.

fish & seafood

spicy clam chowder

There are many versions of chowder, including creamy New England style, tomato-based Manhattan style and dozens of variants all around the world. The name chowder probably came from *chaudière*, a French word for a large iron cooking pot, possibly via the French settlers in Canada. Clam chowders, such as this one, orginated in Boston. If you can't get hold of live clams, use canned ones and add them at the end of the cooking time.

Heat half the olive oil in a large frying pan, add the bacon and sauté until crisp. Remove with a slotted spoon. Add the clams and half the stock. Cover the pan and bring to the boil. Reduce the heat and simmer for 5 minutes or until the clams open.

Put wet muslin or wet kitchen paper in a sieve and pour the clams and their liquid through the sieve to strain out the sand. Reserve the cooking liquid and the clams.

Heat the remaining olive oil in the rinsed pan, add the onion, potatoes, celery, paprika and chilli and sauté for 5 minutes. Add the tomatoes, remaining stock and salt flakes. Bring to the boil, reduce the heat and simmer for 10 minutes or until the vegetables are part-tender. Add the reserved cooking liquid, bacon and clams, stir gently, then simmer for 5–10 minutes until the flavours are well blended. Serve in deep, wide soup bowls, with parsley sprinkled on top.

Note Saltines (salted, crisp crackers) are the traditional accompaniment for this chowder, but any salted crackers will do. French bread or crusty rolls are also suitable.

4 tablespoons extra virgin olive oil

4 slices bacon, cut into strips or large dice, about 75 g

1 kg live long-neck clams or other clams, well scrubbed

750 ml boiling Fish or Chicken Stock (pages 8–9)

1 large onion, chopped

2–4 medium potatoes, cubed, about 400 g

3 celery stalks, sliced

2 teaspoons hot paprika

1 medium-hot red chilli, deseeded and chopped

400 g canned chopped tomatoes

1 teaspoon sea salt flakes

leaves from 1 small bunch of flat leaf parsley, chopped

serves 6–8

basque fish soup

France has many fish soups but only this one includes hot chillies. The advantages of this recipe are that it can be made successfully without hard-to-come-by Mediterranean fish and it is also quick to make. The bones and prawn shells add flavour, as well as making it a bit messy, but this is fishermen's fare, so roll up your sleeves and enjoy.

Heat the olive oil in a stockpot. Add the pepper and onion and cook until browned, about 5 minutes. Stir in the garlic, chilli, paprika, thyme and tomatoes and cook for 5 minutes more.

Add the fish stock, monkfish, hake and prawns to the stockpot. Bring to the boil, skim off the foam and simmer gently until the fish is cooked through, 10–15 minutes.

Meanwhile, to make the garlic croutons, arrange the baguette slices in a single layer on a baking sheet. Bake in a preheated oven at 180°C (350°F) Gas 4 until golden, 5–8 minutes. Let cool slightly, then rub with the garlic cloves and set aside.

Pour the wine into a large saucepan, cover and bring to the boil for 1 minute, then remove from the heat. Add the prepared mussels to the wine, cover and steam over high heat until just opened, 2–3 minutes. Remove the mussels from their shells, discarding any that do not open.

Add the mussels and cooking liquid to the soup and stir well. Sprinkle with parsley and serve immediately, with the garlic croutons.

*Note To prepare mussels, start 15 minutes before you are ready to use them. Rinse them in cold water and tap any open ones against the work surface. If they don't close, discard them. Scrub the others with a stiff brush and scrape off any barnacles. Pull off and discard the wiry beards.

2 tablespoons extra virgin olive oil

1 red pepper, halved, deseeded and sliced

1 onion, halved and sliced

3 garlic cloves, crushed

1 green chilli, deseeded and chopped

¼ teaspoon best-quality hot paprika

a sprig of thyme

225 g canned chopped peeled tomatoes

1.5 litres Fish Stock (page 9)

250 g monkfish fillet, cut into bite-sized pieces

500 g hake or cod steaks

250 g unpeeled prawn tails

250 ml dry white wine

500 g fresh mussels*

a handful of flat leaf parsley, chopped

garlic croutons

1 baguette, sliced

2 garlic cloves

serves 4–6

grilled salmon noodle soup

Given some fresh salmon steaks and a kitchen stocked with some pretty basic Asian ingredients, this elegant dinner dish can be on the table in about 8 minutes – 30 if you're chatting and enjoying yourself over a glass of wine. Add whatever vegetables you have on hand and if you prefer wheat-free noodles, you can substitute rice noodles or cellophane noodles.

1 tub silken tofu

2 bundles somen or soba noodles

4 large salmon steaks, skin on

2 tablespoons sunflower oil

1 litre dashi stock powder and water

your choice of other vegetables, such as sugar snap peas (a large handful per serving)

a handful of Chinese dried mushrooms, such as tree ear, soaked in hot water for 20 minutes

about 6 spring onions, sliced

sea salt, fish sauce or soy sauce, to taste (optional)

freshly sliced chillies or chilli sauce, to taste (optional)

a ridged stove-top grill pan (optional)

serves 4

To prepare the tofu, put it between 2 plates and put a weight on top of the plates. This will force out some of the liquid and make it stick together better. Just before serving, cut into about 12 cubes by making 3 cuts one way and 4 cuts the other.

Bring a large saucepan of water to the boil and add the noodles. Have a glass of cold water ready. When the water comes to the boil, add a dash of cold water. When it returns to the boil, do it again, let it return to the boil and do it again. This will help to cook the noodles perfectly right to the middle – the cold water 'frightens' the heat into the interior. Test after 3–4 minutes, then drain and keep in cold water until ready to serve.

Put the salmon in a plastic bag, then add the oil and toss to coat. Bring a ridged stove-top grill pan or frying pan to a high heat, then remove the salmon from the bag and add it to the pan, skin side down. When the skin is charred and the flesh has turned pale about 1 cm through, turn the salmon over and lightly sear the other side.

Bring the dashi to the boil, then lightly blanch your chosen vegetables. Remove with a slotted spoon. Drain the mushrooms and slice into pieces, discarding the hard stalk tips.

Put a pile of drained noodles into each bowl. Put the salmon steaks, skin side up, on top. Add the tofu cubes, mushrooms and any other vegetables used. Ladle the stock over the top and serve topped with spring onions. If you prefer, add seasoning in the form of salt, soy sauce or fish sauce and fire in the form of fresh chillies or chilli sauce.

hot and sour soup

Almost everyone in South-east Asia has a version of this soup. Interestingly, it is the pineapple and tomatoes as well as the obvious tamarind that are seen as the sour part of the soup. The beansprouts and spring onions can be served separately along with the kumquats, herbs and spices so that people can add them according to taste.

Put the stock in a large saucepan, add the lemongrass, chillies, tamarind paste and/or pineapple, fish sauce and sugar. Bring to the boil and simmer for about 5 minutes. Add the tomatoes, then taste and adjust the seasoning with more fish sauce or sugar, as you like.

Add the fish and simmer for a few minutes until the flesh is opaque. Add the prawns and simmer until they are opaque and pink at the edges. Don't overcook or you will lose the flavour.

Put the beansprouts and spring onions into soup bowls, then add the fish and prawns and handfuls of herbs. Ladle the broth over the top. Serve with little dishes of salt, pepper, kumquats, fish sauce, chillies and extra herbs.

Variation For a more substantial meal, you can add cooked rice noodles or cellophane noodles to the bowls before the beansprouts.

1 litre Fish Stock (page 9) or water

3 fresh stalks of lemongrass, halved and crushed

2 red chillies, deseeded and halved

1 tablespoon tamarind paste and/or 2 slices small pineapple, cut into wedges

3 tablespoons fish sauce, plus extra to taste

1 tablespoon sugar, plus extra to taste

2 small tomatoes, preferably unripe, cut into wedges

about 500 g fish, such as small kingfish, huss or ribbonfish, cut crossways into 4 cm steaks, or fillets

4–8 shelled medium uncooked prawns, with tail fins intact

a handful of fresh beansprouts, trimmed, rinsed and drained

2 spring onions, chopped

4 large handfuls of fresh Asian herbs, such as coriander, mint, sawtooth coriander, Asian basil (but not regular basil), plus extra to serve

to serve

a small dish with a pile each of salt and pepper

a handful of kumquats or 2 limes, halved

a small dish of fish sauce

a small dish of chopped chillies

serves 4

chicken

wonton chicken soup

Delicious wonton fillings take seconds to make in a food processor, and these little Chinese 'ravioli' can be used in soup, steamed and served with sauce, or even deep-fried and served as snacks. You can change the fillings too; pork, shrimp and other seafood are all wonderful.

8 Chinese cabbage leaves

1 cooked chicken breast, shredded

1 carrot, thinly sliced lengthwise, then blanched for 1 minute

2 spring onions, thinly sliced lengthways

a handful of fresh beansprouts, rinsed, drained and trimmed

wontons

125 g pork fillet or chicken breast, sliced

3 spring onions, chopped

a pinch of sea salt

1 teaspoon freshly grated ginger

2 canned water chestnuts, chopped

1 egg white, lightly beaten with a fork

12 small wonton wrappers*

chinese chicken stock

1.5 litres Chicken Stock (page 8)

4 whole star anise

5 cm fresh ginger, peeled and sliced

1 onion, sliced

serves 4

Bring a large saucepan of water to the boil. Add the Chinese cabbage leaves and blanch for 1 minute. Plunge into a bowl of iced water for 5 minutes. Drain, then cut out and discard the white ribs. Put 4 leaves, one on top of the other, on a tea towel. Roll them up into a cylinder and press out the liquid. Cut the cylinder crossways into 3 cm long sections. Repeat with the other 4 leaves, to make little cabbage 'sushi'.

To make the wontons, put the pork in a food processor and pulse until minced. Add the spring onions, salt and ginger and pulse again. Transfer to a bowl and stir in the water chestnuts. Brush a circle of egg white around the centre of each wonton wrapper and put 1 teaspoon of mixture in the middle. Twirl the wrapper around the filling to make a shuttlecock shape. Press to seal.

Put the stock ingredients in a saucepan and simmer for 10 minutes. Strain to remove the flavourings, then return the stock to the rinsed pan. Reheat the stock, add the wontons and poach them for 1½ minutes – they will rise to the surface like fresh pasta (which is what they are). Divide the wontons, stock, cabbage rolls, chicken and carrot between heated soup plates, top with the spring onions and beansprouts and serve.

*Note You can buy wonton wrappers or 'skins' either chilled or frozen in Chinese supermarkets. You peel off as many as you need, then the leftovers can be wrapped and kept frozen for later use.

chicken soup with vegetables

The basis of this soup is the simplest, best, most flavourful chicken soup in the world, an Asian stock even more wonderful than the legendary Jewish mother's chicken soup. The better the chicken, the better the stock, so invest in organic, kosher, free-range and all those desirable things.

Put all the chicken stock ingredients in a large saucepan, add water to cover the chicken by 3 cm, bring to the boil, reduce the heat and simmer for at least 1 hour.

Remove the chicken, whole, from the pan and reserve. Scoop out the solids from the stock, reserving the ginger. Put the ginger on a plate and cut into tiny slivers.

Strain the stock into a saucepan, ladling at first, then pouring through muslin. It should be clear but slightly fatty on top, although you may wish to blot off some of the excess fat.

Taste the stock and reduce if necessary. Season to taste. Pull shreds of chicken off the bird and cut into bite-sized pieces if necessary. Put in a bowl and cover.

Return the stock to the boil, add the ginger slivers and the thick parts of the asparagus and blanch for 30 seconds. Add the asparagus tips and blanch for 3 seconds more. Add the peas, tomatoes and chicken and blanch for 30 seconds. You are heating them and keeping the peas and tomatoes fresh, rather than cooking them to a mush. Ladle into large soup bowls and top with sliced chilli and the herb of your choice. Cooked noodles may also be added.

a handful of mini asparagus tips, halved crossways

a large handful of sugar snap peas, cut into 2–3 pieces each

1 punnet cherry tomatoes, quartered and deseeded

sea salt and freshly ground black pepper

south-east asian chicken stock

1 small organic chicken

2 whole star anise

2 cinnamon sticks

a handful of kaffir lime leaves

2 stalks of lemongrass, halved lengthways and bruised

7 cm ginger, peeled and sliced

4 garlic cloves, lightly crushed but whole

1 red chilli, halved lengthways

1 tablespoon peppercorns, bruised

to serve

1 red or green chilli, sliced

fresh coriander, Chinese chives, parsley, chives or other herbs

cooked noodles (optional)

serves 4

laksa

3 tablespoons peanut oil

500 ml canned coconut milk

2 boneless chicken breasts, skinned and thickly sliced

fish sauce or sea salt, to taste

750 g fresh or 100 g dried udon noodles

spice paste

3–6 red or orange chillies, cored and chopped

1 shallot, chopped

2 stalks of lemongrass, thinly sliced

3 cm fresh ginger, thinly sliced

½ teaspoon ground turmeric

6 blanched almonds, chopped

1 tablespoon fish sauce or a pinch of sea salt

1 garlic clove, crushed

to serve

250 g fresh beansprouts, trimmed, rinsed and drained

4 spring onions, sliced diagonally

1 red chilli, cored and thinly sliced

sprigs of fresh coriander (optional)

serves 4

Laksas are spicy soups from Malaysia, Indonesia and the Philippines, though the Malay ones are the best known. They usually contain vegetables, prawns, pork and noodles, but this varies from region to region. This one contains chicken, but you can ring the changes with fish and other seafood instead. The spice paste is the key and although it is usually laboriously made with a mortar and pestle, a food processor is an easy, modern alternative.

Put all the spice paste ingredients into a spice grinder or a small food processor and work to a paste, adding a little water if necessary. Alternatively, use a mortar and pestle.

Heat the oil in a wok, then add the spice paste and cook gently for about 5 minutes until aromatic. Add the thick part of the coconut milk (if any) and stir-fry until it throws out its oil, then add the thinner part and heat gently. Add 1 litre water and bring to the boil. Add the chicken, reduce the heat and poach gently without boiling until the chicken is cooked through, about 10–15 minutes. Add fish sauce, to taste.

If using fresh noodles, rinse in cold water, then boil for about 1–2 minutes. If using dried noodles, cook in boiling unsalted water for 3–5 minutes, or until done, then drain. Divide the noodles between large soup bowls. Add the chicken and liquid, top with the beansprouts, spring onions, chilli and coriander, if using, and serve.

goan chicken soup

Indians don't go in for soup – unless it's a remnant of some kind of colonial rule, as this one is. The Portuguese were so loath to give up their colonies when India gained independence in 1947 that it took another 20 years for them to be persuaded to leave Goa. Now, Christian Goa is the only place in India that you'll find beef and pork dishes, but chicken is acceptable to everyone except strict vegetarians.

Heat the oil in a saucepan, add the onion, garlic and ginger and fry gently until softened but not browned. Add the rice, turmeric and stock and season with salt and pepper. Simmer for 10 minutes, then add the peas and chicken and simmer until the rice is soft, about another 10 minutes.

To make the tempered topping (a favourite garnish in India), heat the oil in a wok or frying pan, add the mustard seeds and stir-fry until they pop. Add the garlic and stir-fry until crisp. Take care, because it can easily burn and burnt garlic is bitter. Remove with a slotted spoon and set aside. Add the onions and stir-fry at a low temperature until well covered with the oil. Continue cooking until tender. Add the curry leaves, if using, and cook for a few minutes until aromatic. Return the garlic to the mixture and remove from the heat.

To serve, ladle the soup into bowls, then top with the tempered mixture.

Note Basmati rice is the most delicate of rice varieties, and should be handled gently because the grains can break easily.

1 tablespoon peanut oil or ghee

1 onion, finely chopped

3 garlic cloves, crushed

3 cm fresh ginger, peeled and grated

125 g rice, preferably basmati

½ teaspoon ground turmeric

1 litre Chicken Stock (page 8)

100 g shelled green peas

500 g cooked chicken, shredded into bite-sized pieces

sea salt and freshly ground black pepper

tempered topping

2 tablespoons peanut oil or ghee

1 tablespoon mustard seeds

2–4 garlic cloves, thinly sliced

3 small yellow onions, thinly sliced

a handful of curry leaves (optional)

serves 4

meat

vietnamese beef noodle soup (pho bo)

Pho bo, or beef soup, is probably the most famous dish to come out of Vietnam, one of the great classics. It is eaten mainly for breakfast, but you can find it almost any time of day. It is a wonderful combination of fresh herbs, full-flavoured stock, aromatic spices and deliciously filling noodles. *Pho* is pronounced 'far', and there are also chicken and vegetarian versions, though beef is best.

To make the Vietnamese beef stock, put all the stock ingredients in a saucepan, bring to the boil and simmer for 30 minutes. Keep hot.

Meanwhile, if using dried noodles, put them in a bowl and cover with hot water. Let soak for about 15 minutes, then drain and keep in a bowl of cold water until ready to serve. If using fresh noodles, cut or separate them into strips, rinse in hot water for a few minutes, then keep in a bowl of cold water until ready to serve.

Blanch the onion in boiling water for 2 minutes. Drain the noodles, dip in a saucepan of boiling water for a minute or so until hot, then divide between big soup bowls. Add the chillies and blanched onion, then put the sliced beef on top. Return the beef stock to the boil, then strain it into the bowls.

Serve the lime wedges, beansprouts, fresh herbs, chillies and Asian fish sauce separately.

*Note Vietnamese basil is available in Asian stores. Do not use ordinary basil – omit it if you can't find the real thing.

4 bundles dried broad rice noodles or cellophane noodles or 2 packets fresh rice noodles

1 onion, halved and thinly sliced

2–4 hot red chillies, deseeded if you like, but thinly sliced, plus extra to serve

250 g rump or fillet steak, very thinly sliced (freezing it first will make it easier to slice)

easy vietnamese beef stock

1½ litres Beef Stock (page 8)

3–4 onions, thinly sliced

3 cm fresh ginger, sliced

8 whole star anise

½ unwaxed lime or lemon, with skin, sliced

1 tablespoon Asian fish sauce

1 teaspoon sugar

to serve

2 limes, quartered

4 handfuls of fresh beansprouts, rinsed, drained and trimmed

a large bunch of coriander

a large bunch of Vietnamese basil*

a large bunch of Vietnamese mint or ordinary mint

75 ml Asian fish sauce

serves 4

indonesian beef and coconut soup

750 g trimmed braising beef, cut into small chunks

7 white peppercorns

3 cm fresh galangal or ginger, peeled and sliced

1 teaspoon freshly grated nutmeg

¼ teaspoon ground turmeric

325 ml coconut milk

sea salt

plain rice, to serve

spice paste

2–3 tablespoons peanut oil

1 teaspoon ground coriander

7 white peppercorns

4 red bird's eye chillies

2 teaspoons brown sugar

1 garlic clove, chopped

5 fresh Thai basil (or sweet basil) leaves

a large handful of fresh coriander, about 25 g, chopped

8 pink Thai shallots or 1 regular shallot

a few cardamom seeds (not pods)

2 cm fresh ginger, peeled and chopped

a small piece of shrimp paste*, toasted in a dry frying pan or the oven, or 1 teaspoon anchovy paste mixed with 1 tablespoon fish sauce

serves 4–6

This strongly spiced and flavoured soup is quintessentially Indonesian in its spicing, influenced by the nation's diverse population and topography. Living on the world's largest archipelago and comprising around 350 ethnic groups, Indonesians are a varied people and so is their cuisine. What comes across in dishes like this soup is a fascinating mixture of spices and flavours.

Put all the spice paste ingredients into a small food processor and grind to a thick paste, adding a dash of water to keep the blades turning if necessary. Set aside.

Put the beef, peppercorns, galangal, nutmeg, turmeric and salt into a saucepan, add 1.5 litres water and bring to the boil, skimming off the foam as it rises to the surface. Stir, reduce the heat and simmer uncovered for about 1½ hours, until the meat is tender and the stock is well reduced.

Strain the beef, discarding the galangal slices and peppercorns, but reserving the beef and stock. Return the stock to the pan, then stir in the spice paste. Bring to the boil, reduce the heat, add the beef and simmer for 5 minutes, stirring regularly.

Finally, add the coconut milk and simmer gently for a few minutes. Serve the soup on its own or with a small mound of plain rice.

*Note Dried shrimp paste is also known as trassi, beluchan or blachan. Extremely pungent, it gives a distinctive taste to South-east Asian food and is worth hunting down in a Thai/Malay/Indonesian food store. Use a very small piece (about ½ teaspoon) and always toast it before using. Wrap it in foil and toast it in a hot oven until it darkens – a few minutes per side.

sausage soup

A deliciously simple soup from the south of France. Use all-meat sausages if you can find them. Pouring the soup over the cheese-topped croutes is very traditionally French, although you can serve them separately if you prefer. This serves four as a simple winter supper, but can be made more substantial by adding extra vegetables, as suggested in the note below.

Arrange the sausages in a ring around a large, shallow, flameproof casserole dish or baking dish. Put the onions and tomatoes in the middle and sprinkle with olive oil. Cook in a preheated oven at 200°C (400°F) Gas 6 until done (about 30 minutes, depending on the thickness of the sausages). Stir the onions and tomatoes after 15–20 minutes to stop them burning.

When the sausages are done, remove, cut into 3–4 pieces each and set aside. Put the dish on top of the stove and add the pancetta. Fry, stirring, until crisp, and the fat is starting to run. Add the garlic and fry for about 1 minute, then add the sage. Add about 1 litre water and stir. Taste and adjust the seasoning, adding extra water if the mixture is too thick.

Meanwhile, put the slices of baguette on a baking sheet and cook at the top of the oven until golden brown. Remove from the oven and sprinkle with grated cheese. Return to the oven until the cheese has melted and become almost crisp.

To serve, put about 3 cheese-topped croutes in 4 soup plates, ladle in the soup and top with the sausages. Sprinkle with parsley, if using, and serve.

Note The bacon may be omitted, but the soup will need more seasoning. Other vegetables, such as quartered and sliced courgettes or cabbage, may also be used.

16 thin pork sausages, pricked with a fork

3 onions, chopped

3 tomatoes, skinned, deseeded and chopped

250 g smoked pancetta or streaky bacon, chopped

2 garlic cloves, crushed with a pinch of sea salt

a large sprig of sage, sliced

1 baguette, sliced

250 g cheese, such as Cheddar, coarsely grated

sea salt and freshly ground black pepper

olive oil, for sprinkling

chopped fresh parsley, to serve (optional)

serves 4

cabbage soup

A classic case of less is more. This soup is soothing and restorative, and deliciously delicate, despite its rustic origins. Homemade salt pork makes all the difference to the taste and is very simple to do yourself. You will have to sacrifice some refrigerator space for three days, which is the only complication, but you will be well rewarded. Your butcher should be able to supply the pickling salt.

750 g pork belly, sliced

100 g pickling salt

1 onion, studded with a clove

1 fresh bay leaf

1 cabbage

1 inner celery stalk with leaves, cut into chunks

7 carrots, cut into chunks

4 turnips, cut into chunks

1 tablespoon unsalted butter, plus extra to serve

750 g small new potatoes, peeled

coarse sea salt and freshly ground black pepper

country bread, thickly sliced, to serve

serves 4–6

Three days before you plan to serve the soup, put the pork belly slices in a shallow ceramic or glass dish and add water to cover. Add the salt and stir until dissolved. Cover and refrigerate for 3 days, turning occasionally. Alternatively, ask a butcher to salt the pork belly for you.

The day of serving, remove the pork belly from its brine and rinse. Put the pork and onion in a large saucepan with 3 litres water. Bring to the boil and skim off any foam that rises to the surface. Reduce the heat, cover and let simmer. Meanwhile, bring another saucepan of water to the boil with the bay leaf. When it boils, add the cabbage and blanch for 5 minutes. Remove the cabbage and drain. When cool enough to handle, slice the cabbage.

Add the sliced cabbage, celery, carrots, turnips and butter to the pork. Taste for seasoning; it may not even need salt because of the salt pork. Return to the boil, then lower the heat, cover and simmer for about 30 minutes. Taste for seasoning again.

Add the potatoes and cook until they are tender, 20–25 minutes more. To serve, remove the pork belly and cut into bite-sized pieces. Trim off any rind and discard any bones. Return the pork pieces to the soup and sprinkle with black pepper. Serve hot, with a spoonful of butter in each bowl and thick slices of country bread.

Note If you don't have time to salt the pork yourself, buy a smoked pork knuckle and proceed as in the main recipe.

cajun-spiced chowder with corn and bacon

Chowders are creamy, chunky soups, the most famous of which is New England clam chowder (see also page 39). Corn chowders are popular too – a real taste of America. This version takes inspiration from the Deep South and the result is Louisiana soul food with just the right amount of Acadian (Cajun country) spice.

4 ears of corn or 475 g fresh or frozen kernels

25 g butter

1 onion, finely chopped

1 small celery stalk, finely chopped

4–5 slices back bacon, chopped

1.25 litres Vegetable Stock (page 9)

250 ml single cream

crusty bread, to serve

Cajun spice blend

¼ teaspoon black peppercorns

¼ teaspoon white peppercorns

½ teaspoon cumin seeds

½ teaspoon coriander seeds

½ teaspoon cayenne pepper

½ teaspoon paprika

½ teaspoon celery salt

serves 4

To make the Cajun spice blend, crush the peppercorns and seeds with a mortar and pestle until coarsely ground. Add the cayenne, paprika and celery salt and mix well.

If using fresh ears of corn, remove the husks and silks and cut the stalk end flat. Put the flat end on a board and cut off the kernels from top to bottom. Discard the cobs.

Melt the butter in a large saucepan, add the onion and sauté for 5 minutes. Add the celery and sauté for a further 3 minutes until well softened. Add the bacon and cook for 1–2 minutes. Add the corn and 1½ teaspoons Cajun spice blend and mix well.

Add the stock and bring to the boil. Reduce the heat and simmer for about 35 minutes. Add the cream and simmer until thickened. You can serve the soup immediately, or, to thicken it further, put a ladle of the chowder (without any of the bacon) into a food processor and purée until smooth. Pour the blended chowder back into the saucepan and mix well.

To serve, ladle into bowls and top with a light dusting of Cajun spice blend. Serve hot with crusty bread.

index

recipe credits

Maxine Clark
Pages 19, 27, 35

Clare Ferguson
Page 39

Manisha Gambhir Harkins
Pages 36, 57, 62

Elsa Petersen-Schepelern
Pages 8, 9, 11, 23, 29, 31, 32,
43, 44, 47, 48, 51, 52, 55, 58

Laura Washburn
Pages 12, 15, 16, 20, 24, 40, 61

photography credits

Peter Cassidy
Endpapers, pages 1, 2, 6 right, 7,
10, 22, 29, 30, 33, 37, 38, 42, 45,
46, 49, 50, 53, 54, 56, 59, 63

Martin Brigdale
Pages 4–5, 6 below left, 13, 14,
18, 21, 26, 34, 41, 60

David Munns
Pages 17, 25

Christopher Drake
Page 6 above left